The Road to Downpatrick

A never forgotten visit... Donal McCormick

The geolocations of many of the sites around North Mayo, mentioned in the above chapters, can be easily located by accessing dunbriste.com

Introduction

This story was put on paper at least seven years ago. As the writer approached his eightieth birthday he realised that what he knew and loved about where he was born and reared, would be largely unknown by his and other people's grandchildren, and indeed by the general visitors to the area. Unfinished it was put away on the shelf, until the arrival of the Wild Atlantic Way prompted its revival.

It is no surprise that the story he had pictured has been, in much of the detail, the route which the inspired concept of the Wild Atlantic Way has followed. And so he hopes that you as 'Other people's grandchildren' will, as you travel his roamings, enjoy the road to Downpatrick too.

Childhood memories draw me back time and again to the marvellous place that is Downpatrick. It is rare to find concentrated in such a small area, so many features as are to be found in it. This is also true of the journey through the surrounding parishes as you make your way there.

The Head is crowned by the magnificent stack of Dún Briste; the rock formation laid down aeons ago and formed and carved out over the centuries. This has left many unique geological features in Downpatrick, or the Down as it is known locally.

Then you have in the fifth century, St Patrick's arrival to this whole area of Mayo. He relates of being called to 'The western seaboard' in his writings and is recorded in the folklore of the region. In 1393 the 'Annals of the Four Master's record what is probably the history of Dún Briste's formation.

In 1798 the last invasion of Ireland took place in this very locality that we can visit, when the French under General Humbert landed at Kilcummin, a few miles north of Killala while in the 20th century, World War II left its mark visibly on the head.

It is hoped that some of the following writings will enliven your journey, with a lot more detail and with pictures of times old and new from the area.

ERECTED BY THE
VOLUNTARY SUBSCRIPTIONS OF
THE PRIESTS AND PEOPLE
OF MAYO AND SLIGO.
IN MEMORY OF
GENERAL HUMBERT
SARRAZIN, LOUIS OCTAVE FONTAINE
BARTHOLOMEW TEELING, MATTHEW TONE
HENRY O'KEON, FATHER CONROY
PATRICK WALSH
AND THE OTHER GALLANT PATRIOTS
WHO SACRIFICED THEIR LIVES
FOR THE FREEDOM OF THEIR COUNTRY
AFTER THE LANDING OF THE FRENCH
UNVEILED BY
MAUD GONNE MACBRIDE 1898
RE DEDICATED BY
SEAN MACBRIDE S.C.
21ST AUGUST 1987

Starting from Ballina

So our narrative of history and folklore, local information and stories starts here, and no better place in Ballina than the Monument to General Humbert, who figures largely in the annals of North Mayo. He was the leader and inspiration of the expedition which landed at Kilcummin with a force of 1,100 French soldiers.

His story is told in more depth when we visit that part of Mayo. Ballina however has honoured him with a monument, in the street named after him namely Humbert Street. It depicts Mother Ireland and is on the route near the roundabout signed for Sligo. It is a useful point from which we can start our exploration of this historical and beautiful part of Mayo.

Leaving the Monument, we travel on the R314 towards the town centre, take the first exit at the roundabout, go past the Town Council Offices and go straight on where it is signed for Belleek. Continue until the Belleek Castle Gatehouse appears, again on your left. It is an imposing building and gives a hint of what a visit to Belleek Castle promises. So travelling through the gate-lodge and taking a sharp right, with the marked athletic running lanes on your left and parking there, you are at the start of a walk way down along the Moy estuary. This is now the planned start of the 'Monasteries of the Moy' Greenway being developed between Killala and Ballina of which more later. The pathway brings us through Belleek woods which has several fascinating prepared walks, which are pram and wheelchair friendly.

↖ Left: Humbert Monument, Ballina.

← Far left: 1798 re-enactment in Ballina

These are mapped out for you to explore. Another car park marks the end of this walk and it can be picked up later, when travelling the route known as the French Road which we come to in the Chapter marked 'The Abbeys and Bartra Island'. So back to where we entered at the gate lodge and passing the athletic track on the right, Belleek Woods comes up and here is another place to leave the car. This is possibly the best spot to explore the woods. Keep your eyes open, for dedicated nature lovers have established a colony of red squirrel and you may surprise them before they scamper away. Established several years ago, the squirrels have spread to Drummin wood near Pontoon and to the vicinity of Crossmolina. Their grey cousins have apparently never managed to cross the Shannon and so the venture of this establishment is a great boost to the lovable red species. There is a picnic spot where you may leave your vehicle if you go on the lookout for them and other features of this interesting spot.

To Belleek

Travelling on, a signpost points the way to Belleek Castle itself. Originally built in the 1820s by the Knox Gore family (whose relatives built many fine residences in the area, most of which have now disappeared) it has had a chequered history. Bought by Isaac Beckett Sawmills Co. from the town, when shipping timber in to the Quay became impossible because of World War II, the mature forest of suitable lumber value was felled and must have been replanted. I have recently learned a little bit of history in this regard.

In 1927 a violent storm caused the sailing ship named SINE to drag her anchors and be wrecked on the seaward side of Bartra Island. She had loaded a cargo of lumber in Gothenburg in western Sweden, which was consigned for landing on Ballina Quay for the same Isaac Beckett. I would presume payment was due when safely landed on the Quay, as the consignee had, after the wreck, to buy the timber from the insurers for a sum of £2,000. This had to include the now worthless, foundered shipwreck. Many years later, the present owners of Belleek Castle on being able to prove ownership of the wreck, were able to rescue from the island owners, many suitable pieces of timber for internal fitting in the castle. More mention of Bartra comes up later in our journey.

After the war years, the Castle was renovated as a sanatorium, for the treatment and curing of tuberculosis. This was a dreaded scourge at the time. With the advent of streptomycin and other drugs, this disease was virtually conquered and thankfully the Castle became redundant for that purpose. It was then bought by the Doran family from Jersey, who brought the skills of hotel management to it. With enterprise they totally refurbished it and have over the years developed it into a luxury hotel, with further development of the premises ongoing. The great entrance hall has the original ceiling, as have other rooms, showing beautiful workmanship. The owner plans to develop the courtyard with a coffee shop and from there take visitors on a tour of both outside, and inside to the Great Banquet Hall which has beautiful timber carvings gathered from different world sources.

Then there is the Museum where artefacts collected by the present owner's father have been assembled in a unique display. This is no ordinary undertaking and you should not miss it. With the reputed bedroom of Gráinne Úaile, which came from Westport House which was her base, including her four poster bed, and the Marshal Doran Collection which ranges from a rock slice of dinosaur fossil to numerous other specimen rocks to be seen, Belleek is certainly full of wonder and amazement. In the 'armoury' dating from the last early millennium he has put together an unbelievable collection of pre-gunpowder era weaponry. To see the small size of some of the armour shows how mankind has grown since those times.

↖ The Armoury, Belleek Castle.

← Left: Bar in Belleek Castle.

← Far left: Grace O'Malley's bed at Belleek Castle.

The Abbeys & Bartra Island

Leaving the Castle, turn right at the signed junction and pass the remnants of what was the farmyard of the estate; just part of the old cut-stone retaining wall remains. When you read this, the planned reopening of the estate's vegetable walled-garden may have taken place. This road takes you past the Belleek caravan and camping site (perhaps useful to know) and onwards you come to the R314 main road. You turn right and here there is a choice, for this road brings you to Killala.

Alternatively, driving on it for half a kilometre or so and again turning right and following a twisty rural road, watch out, for after a few kilometres a sign will point you to Rosserk Friary ruins, and further on to Moyne Abbey. The Friary, one of the best preserved Franciscan ruins in the country, was founded around 1440 and burnt down in 1590 like many others by, allegedly, Sir Richard Bingham, Elizabeth I soldier in the country, in reforming zeal at the time. One of the features of the building that has fascinated me was how the square tower was built over four arches, a substantial weight to be carried. The strength of buildings before the days of cement has always amazed me, as lime mortar was, one would think, not as strong. Its gift is however, that it can expand and contract without cracking when hot or cold. Concrete under the same conditions will crack. Here however, it has done a superb job, lasting hundreds of years. Built on the banks of the river Moy, it is well worth exploring.

So we retrace our travels back to where we turned in at the Friary sign and turning right, till after a few kilometres, the road rises and a view of the Moy estuary, Killala Bay and Bartra Island unfolds. Owned by a retired sea captain, back in the 19th century, Captain Kirkwood built an imposing house and on his death, he was buried on the island. He had married and the only family I can trace were twins, Maude and Claude. The male of the two remained in ownership of the island but never married, while his sister moved to Dublin.

Then a Captain Verner, demobbed from military service, bought it from him and started a Guest House aided by his wife, as well as farming the land. However his health broke down and the couple sold it to her twin sister, Joyce Redman, a famous actress who played opposite Sir Lawrence Olivier in the Old Vic Theatre and on tour to New York and onwards. She and her husband holidayed there. Eventually it was sold again, to be a luxury medical centre, but the problem of access across the tidal waters (vehicles could drive and one could walk across

at low spring tides) was always a problem and helped to make it unsuccessful. Then a luxury golf course was planned by a consortium, with world famous golfer Nick Faldo involved. Planning permission was not forthcoming and there the matter lies. It would have been a fantastic venue for a links course. Bartra has always been a spot where boat owners coming down the Moy picnicked and camped on the island. Sadly, a few of the mostly well- behaved visitors vandalised the house after it had been restored. This happened on two occasions.

So leaving that view, the tower of Moyne Abbey comes onto the horizon. Consecrated in 1462, one hundred and twenty-eight years later it was tragically burned along with so many other ecclesiastical established settlements. Moyne is one of the best of these in Mayo and access to it deserves to be developed. It has extensive buildings and, as I remember, even a stream running through the secular parts, a feature which had many uses I would guess. There is a fine view to be had from the tower, which I climbed as a youngster, but for safety reasons this is not now allowed.

The Greenway

Journeying on we re-join the R314 and see where the soon to be opened Greenway crosses the road.

This Greenway, which is being developed, will be a really valuable amenity not only to visitors, but for the whole community. Starting in Killala town from the foot of the Round Tower, the Greenway crosses the road with the Cathedral on your left and the chemist on the right. Then it cuts through ancient walls, through the town park and the old farmyard of the Miller estate, to emerge in the magical woodlands of beech, birch, holly and other evergreens. Then, winding its way, with birdsong to listen to and numerous wild flowers to provide bee life with honey, it is a fascinating walk or cycle ride. On the right-hand side the newly built equine exercise track has been constructed, another point of interest. Carrying on then, it skirts on your left, grassland and the avenue to the mansion. Interestingly, the original building was owned by a Miss Gore who was related to the Knox-Gore family; constructors of Belleek Castle.

The now entrance to the Coca-Cola plant in Ballina, built on part of the Belleek estate, was opened as an avenue for Miss Gore's convenience to shorten her journey when visiting. To get back to the Greenway which, on reaching the road, turns sharp right passing in front of factories and on round the corner where it crosses the road. A causeway has been built across and beside the wetlands, reaching to go under the old railway bridge. With the fortnightly cycle of spring tides, this spot becomes at high tide, nearly flooded by sea water. The railway which closed in the early thirties provides the level route for half a kilometre or so, and then turning left enters another wetland area, a magical spot where wildlife such as duck, heron and moorhen are likely to be seen. Leaving that it joins the road near Moyne Abbey. As yet the next section has not been started.

More History at Killala

Now we return to the signposting for Killala, Ballycastle and onwards. It used to be a problem to describe and guide the journey. Now you just follow the WILD ATLANTIC WAY signs. Killala is a historic old place with ruins of several old corn stores, dating from when grain was exported by sailing ships, before the channel became impassable. Old lore says that the Monks of Rosserk Abbey built a barrier across the river Moy at Bartra island and diverted it to its present channel.

↖ Bartra Island in the foreground and the Ox Mountains behind it

It was said that the plan was to leave the Monks of Moyne Abbey without their supply of salmon, for which the Moy was and is famous. However, it also left Killala without a port of note as the flow of water was too reduced for sailing ships to manoeuvre and navigate. Killala port is now a base for a very efficient and well equipped inshore, semi-inflatable life-boat branch of the Irish Coastguard. They share responsibility for the North Mayo coast with the Ballyglass Ocean going RNLI lifeboat sited north of Belmullet. They also cover the Sligo coast for many miles.

The area around the town has a history of farmer go-ahead. It resulted in the early fifties in the supplying of milk for pasteurising at the formation of Ballina Milk Company. Before that the available volume was very scarce and except for two recognised dairy farms supplying Ballina, it was, like in most towns at the

time, of poor quality and nearly non-existent. The next bit of progress was the opening of Palmerstown Co-operative, started in the late fifties. This brought the opportunity for many farmers to start milk production, supplied to the branch collection creamery near the bridge of that name. The Co-Op then started a supply store for farm needs in Killala, in what was one of the old grain stores. This was on the Quay and seeing the need for fertiliser the farmers had the inspiration of opening the port again and taking in ship loads of Basic Slag, a necessity for productive farming. There was great excitement when the local Dean Ashton piloted in the first ship. Being a keen sailor he knew the navigation marks of the bar. Thus was the tradition of the old port revived. That Co-Op eventually became part of Connacht Gold, now Aurivo, which is one of Ireland's bigger Co-Operatives, serving the farming industry from North Donegal, east to Westmeath and south to Galway.

Killala is now a small thriving fishing port, with sea fishing facilities on hire for visitors. For them too, the town has fine supermarkets, fuel filling station, cycle hire, and other facilities. Also available are several opportunities for Pub grub while there is also a restaurant for a full meal. The old Church of Ireland cathedral predates the reformation and parts have 12th century remains. Inside, it has quaint old family box pews, nowadays a rarity and a souterrain, supposed to go to one of the best round towers in Ireland which stands on the highest point of the town and dominates the entire area. On its south side, about one-third of the way up you may notice a slight bulge. This was where a lightning strike damaged the building and was duly repaired. It shows how well the original was built. This tower was reputedly erected by the famous stone mason known all over Ireland by the name of 'Gubaun Saor'. Many folklore legends are told about him so, I relate this one.

DELTIC
Huntress
D800
ECHO

Folklore at Killala

Many years ago the people of Killala (the name means the church of Alaidhe, a local Chieftain and pronounced Auley) wanted the best round tower in the land to be built, so they employed The Gubaun Saor, a famous builder, known all over the country, to build the best.

When it was completed and the final capping stone firmly set in place, the local people quickly took the ladders and scaffolding away so that a better one would not be built. They left The Gubaun Saor perched on top. He was lamenting his plight to all who would listen and yet to no avail. When his wife arrived with his tea, she listened to him for a minute or two and then shouted "for all your skills you're a stupid man". "Unravel the wool of the sock I knitted for you last week and let the end down to me. I can tie a cord to it and a rope to the cord, pull it up and down you come." When his employers saw what was happening, the ladders were not long in being replaced! Another version tells how she shouted up, "It's easier to throw down three stones than put one up." The town's people, quickly realizing her intent, erected the ladders in great haste and the tower was preserved for us to view.

Apparently his wife was the brains behind her successful husband, as the following story shows. It has been said that as a pastime, The Gubaun used to cut firewood in the forest and his wife noticed that he would come home each evening, weak, ravenous and without a bundle of firewood. Eventually he admitted to his wife that in the forest each day, he was being robbed of his midday meal and his fuel by a fearsome giant. "Ah", she responded, "I'll cure that. I'll go to the wood with you tomorrow and sort out this problem." The next day they set out and when

in the wood she got him to drive a wedge into a big log of timber, far enough that it would not split it, but would still make a crack big enough for her purpose. "Now hide", she instructed "and when the giant comes, watch." So he did and shortly afterward his tormenter arrived and saw the poor woman crying and troubled. "What's wrong?" he asked, "I've stuck the wedge in the timber and can't get it out," the wife cunningly replied. No sooner said than done, so the giant put his two hands into the crack and started to pull it apart. Then, as quick as lightening, she knocked the wedge out and 'snap' the timber closes on his fingers. "Now my man come and deal with this rogue," she shouted and out came the Gubaun Saor, to deal with him and become the victor.

Palmerstown and Onwards

As we leave Killala, taking the Ballycastle Road it skirts the estuary of the Owenmore/Palmerstown River, when after a few kilometres, it brings you to a beautiful, old, eleven arched bridge. It is much photographed for its beauty and is an artist's dream.

Just upstream are the remains of an old mill. During the 'emergency' as the Second World War was called, flour and feedstuffs were very scarce and so in this structure, was a water-wheel powered, grinding mill which processed the local home grown grain into flour.

Here you have a choice. If you swing a hard left when you cross the bridge, following the Wild Atlantic Way sign, you can travel on about three-quarters of a mile where there is a right-hand junction. The alternative when you cross the bridge, is to go straight on. Either route will take you to the French Landing country. These roads join up at Foghill crossroads and will bring you to Kilcummin Pier, near the actual site of the Landing.

← The water powered mill

Ballycastle

Straight on at the afore mentioned right hand junction, the road goes towards Ballycastle and in the town you can take the road sign-posted to the right, on to Downpatrick Head.

Before you come to the town however, on your left, is Carracullen hill which has on its top, a mound. This is reputed to be one of the hunting camps of the legendary Fionn MacCumhaill, one of Ireland's famous legendary heroes. There are several other stone placings, also on this hill which must have had Pre Christian Druidic Ballycastle, like virtually all rural towns, has suffered from loss of trade to the bigger urban centres like Ballina. The messy tradition in years gone by of holding cattle sales or fairs on the streets, died a death when auction marts started up. (Incidentally as an aside, Ballina has probably the most modern livestock mart in the country, which has as well as normal dealing, on line viewing for buying or selling of stock). This mart was a relief for Ballycastle in many ways as the farmers quickly changed to the fairer auction system, but it removed cash flow from the locality eventually closing businesses in the town. However, now the town is fighting back. It has a vibrant Arts Centre where you may be fortunate enough to see a world class artist at work. A visit to the craft shop can be rewarding while there is also a nationally awarded for excellence, cottage kitchen restaurant. Then a few kilometres to the west there is the attraction of Céide Fields which is another fascinating story, bringing much appreciated visitors. The development of magnificent Downpatrick is bringing new life to the local B&Bs, some old established and Bord Fáilte recommended. It might be opportune at this point to write of the road to the Interpretive Centre at Céide Fields as at some point you must not miss the wonderful gathering of the information of 5000 year old history which is revealed so cleverly.

↖ The building behind the red van was the proposed hotel for the All Red Route

To Céide Fields and Flax

So when you are leaving town, your route takes you straight down the hill on which Ballycastle is sited, and turning right at the curve at the bottom, there is, if you take it, on the road about a hundred metres on the left, a little bit of local farming history. There on your left is the remains of a flax scutching mill, one of 4 or 5 which were located in North Mayo. Back in the nineteenth century this area was renowned as a spot well suited for growing the crop which produced the flax fibre. This fibre supported the production, by the industry in Northern Ireland, of the fine Irish Linen.

Eventually the distance from that market left it uneconomic to produce the crop and so it ceased to be cultivated. Then during the thirty nine/forty five war, the demand and the price was such that the growing of the crop got a new lease of life.

The old skills were remembered, the retting dams cleaned out and the eye catching, sky-blue flower of the flax or linseed producing plant could be seen on many of the farms. When the crop had produced the seed heads and it was deemed to have grown the maximum length which could have been up to

← Flax or linseed flowers

three feet, or nearly a metre in height, the plant was pulled with roots attached, in order to get every inch of fibre production. It was then tied in sheaves or bundles and stacked to dry out and wither. The sheaves were then submerged for ten days or so to rot the outer vegetation, in a retting pond of dammed up water where it produced a disgusting rotting stink. This smell was there when the sheaves were removed, adhering to clothes and body so it was a most unpopular job and was usually accompanied by a supply of porter to dull the senses. The timing of lifting the sheaves out of the dam was critical, too soon and the skin would not have rotted enough to allow separating at scutching, but worse if too late and the precious fibre would be damaged. There was therefore a window of just a few hours to get the sheaves out perfectly for the scutching mill. As the growing of this crop was revived during the Second World War, that is why I am familiar with its production. My father never grew the crop on our farm, but I can vividly remember the foul smell of the flax dams.

For some reason they always seemed to site them along the road and the sickening odour made you hurry past with a handkerchief pressed to your nose. Anyway, when the sheaves were extracted they were opened and spread out to dry, retied and stacked to dry out. They were then brought to the scutching mills to be rolled and cracked and the dusty vegetation skin removed, ready for the fibre to be shipped up north for further processing and turning into the quality linen of Northern Ireland. The mill of which I speak was not used at this time, and Crossmolina was the nearest for processing. The flax seed also produces by different methods the 'Golden Linseed' so popular as a health food supplement in a totally different process.

BED & BREAKFAST
GUINNESS
Heineken
Ceide House
Ceide House B&B
B&B
TRADITIONAL MUSIC SESSIONS
GUINNESS
BUS
03-MO-2101

Along the Road

Now if we go on up the hill away from the main road (the R314) and take the first right, this road will pass near a site where a passage tomb was opened by archaeologist Rúaidhrí De Valera.

This area of Mayo has a huge number of such megalithic tombs. Proceeding, this road meets again the main road to our destination and crossing the river and travelling uphill it is worth taking another detour to the right, which takes us past the beautifully sited Stella Maris Hotel. Once one of the many Coast Guard Stations erected in the nineteenth century to keep the law and

Ballycastle beach with the hotel in the background

The Stella Maris Hotel

prevent smuggling, they were robustly built and sometimes carried navigation lights.

We have already passed close to one sited at Ross, signposted this side of Killala to the beach there and another at Kilcummin fishing pier, near the spot the French landed in 1798. Another fishing pier lies just a couple of hundred metres past the hotel. It is also becoming popular as a launching point for kayaks exploring the rugged cliff scenery nearby. Fishing for lobster and crab are of course is main occupation at the pier, while when conditions are right, good surfing is popular.

Glenulra - The Glen of The Eagles

Returning to our road (R314) and turning right and again detouring left is Doonfeeny grave yard. It has the second highest ancient standing stone in the country at 22 feet. Back again and another sculpture trail is sited at a double corner S bend on the slope just in front of you.

Next of interest as the road comes to a shallow valley or glen, steeper as it gets near to the sea, what should catch your attention is its name, Glenurla, as it seems to be pronounced today. As a youngster my father knew it as Glenulra. This translates as 'The Glen of the Eagles'. I'm told the record of the last know Golden Eagles in Ireland was in 1912 along the Céide cliffs. Now on the near horizon, your destination, the pyramid crowned building, the Interpretive Centre for Céide Fields, is obvious. When you get there, a fascinating story is waiting for you.

It started 5000 years ago. However that is such an interesting and well told story that I wouldn't attempt to tell it here - so time to retrace our steps to more recent happenings and history.

More Ballycastle

A little known historic fact about Ballycastle was that it was chosen as a stopping point on the transatlantic route to be developed at the start of the 20th century, just when the famous transatlantic services by liners like the ill-fated Titanic started.

↙ Rathfran Abbey

It was called The ALL RED ROUTE. Starting from New York, the transatlantic liners were to arrive in Broadhaven Bay near Belmullet, to a new port to be built there. The passengers and mail were then to be transported by railway, to be built from Belmullet via Glenamoy and Belderrig to Ballycastle and Killala which had a railhead at that time, then on to Dublin, Holyhead and London.

This was to shorten the time by two days for the journey, for both passengers and mail. Radio communication was not then feasible and so shortening communications was apparently necessary and viable. Nowadays nanoseconds are the measurements by which communications are measured and of immense value, which is why the fibre optic cable coming ashore at Ross near Killala will be so valuable. In Ballycastle, on the left, at the top of the town, is the building which was to be a Grand hotel, built in anticipation of the All Red Route. Sadly for the area the whole scheme fell through as communications by radio came on stream. The building has served its time as a Convent and for relief while building and refurbishing of the local second level school, St. Patrick's College, Lacken Cross.

Back to our choice of roads, (in the section Palmerstown and onwards) when the Ballycastle road took our attention, at the mentioned right hand junction you went straight on as you travelled towards Ballycastle, but now if you take that road to the right, signed for Lacken, it is the more scenic route to Downpatrick. However, previous to coming this far, as mentioned earlier, when you cross Palmerstown bridge, by going straight on you have a most interesting route to travel. It is also most historic and scenic. If you are still interested in Abbeys, Rathfran Priory lies just two right turns off this road. It is signposted and you have to walk in by a pathway along the shore to it. Dating from 1274 it was another casualty to the Henry VIII dissolution of the Abbeys. Access is not easy but the main building is sound with several flat tombstones which are semi legible still to be seen. To the west side, the foundations of many rooms are marked with rebuilt mini walls.

The actual flat
rocks where
the French
disembarked
north of
Kilcummin pier

The French Landing 1798

This diversion which we have taken is not actually part of the route set out for the Wild Atlantic Way but it will take you to a beautiful and historic area. Kilcummin is internationally known as a great spot for surfing as is the beach known as the back-strand.

On your way to that beach you will pass one of the Tír Sáile Sculpture Trail monuments, while across the field to the right is possibly the best of these creations. This is Site 'D' on the Tír Sáile Trail and is entitled 'A sanctuary, a place near the pulse of the tide'. Site 'E' lies just before the road turns left and is entitled 'The Echo of Nawascape'.

As you traverse this area on your way to Kilcummin, you will find it is signposted extensively as General Humbert's invasion from France. If you turn right at Foghill crossroads (this would be the third junction since leaving the bridge) it would bring you to the area where in 1798 the French army, under General Humbert, landed with a force of about one thousand one hundred men. The actual site of their landing, on a natural rocky slipway, is shown on the accompanying photo. At that time there was no pier. They were bound from France for Lough Swilly in north Donegal but a storm delayed them and blew them off course. On board was a Mayo sailor and he, knowing the coastline, persuaded the convoy to come ashore north of Kilcummin pier. They moved inland out of sight of the sea, the spot is still called Baile Campa (The town of the camp). There must have been fear of discovery by Crown naval forces to cause the need to hide from ships at sea. From there, the army under General Humbert and backed by local pike men, who flocked to enlist, advanced on Killala and took it, swiftly moving onto Ballina.

↖ Sunset on the back strand

The Campaign

Next, they turned their attention to the English garrison stationed in Castlebar. Sending a diversionary party with carts and noisy kitchen implements rattling and banging by Foxford, Humbert travelled west of Lough Conn over what is called the Windy Gap, south of Bofeenuaun and down on an unsuspecting Castlebar.

Here, when General Humbert met the fearful garrison who had come out to face the reported army coming from Foxford, were caught by surprise. He caused consternation by ordering the French troops to 'adopt open order', spreading out with 5 or 6 feet between each soldier. (Armies at the time were used to standing shoulder by shoulder). When they saw the width of the host, the local garrison believed it to be only the preliminary force and so they turned tail and ran defeated to other garrison towns, some as far as Athenry in Co. Galway. This became known as the 'Races of Castlebar' giving General Humbert a great boost. However, his success with such a small force could not last and he was finally defeated after several engagements, at Ballinamuck in Longford. The French officers were treated fairly and were treated as prisoners of war and sent back to France. The Irish who supported them though were met with stronger treatment. Executions and hangings were conducted as punishment for rebellion. Thus hatred and enmity was fostered. An interesting reminder of that ill-fated expedition still is remembered in the 'French march', a popular marching tune which has been recorded and preserved in the area. Later in this story, we will have further history of this period.

More Folklore

If you now return to Foghill crossroads you are near the area where St Patrick was reputed to have visited the wood of Foghla, now known as Foghill [pronounced Fohill]. This wood is mentioned in his writings, approximately around the year 430, as the place where he heard the voice of a young man from the western seaboard calling to him to teach of God's love and His salvation plan for humanity. Don't look for a wood; it is now farmland.

There is a statue of the saint (see photo) at a 'Holy' well down towards the sea just near the river, whose estuary flows out through that great expanse of sand at low tide, known as Lacken Strand. Again folklore tells the story of why there are never any Salmon caught in that river. The Cloonalaghan (Irish meaning 'the wet meadow of the ducks' or more correctly 'O'Loughlin's meadow') river was apparently an angler's paradise and as the saint walked its banks he met with an old man fishing for Salmon. "Will you give me the next one you catch?" he said. "Indeed I will, and you are welcome to it" the angler replied.

Next thing, the fisherman hooked a really big one and on landing it he was not anxious to part with such a beauty. "Oh" he said. "I'll give you the next one". However, it was even bigger than the last and so again he promised the saint the next. The third one was a prize specimen and again greed took over. St Patrick, seeing this said, "there will never be another one." And neither has there been since.

Lacken and its Strand

So if you leave the French area and return, through Foghill Cross to the 'Wild-Atlantic-Way' signposting and take the left fork at Maughan's pub and shop, (again temporarily leaving the 'Wild-Atlantic-Way' signing) do not be startled by a very lifelike portrait of a French soldier aiding a wounded Irish pikeman.

Looking uphill your eye may notice the monument on top of the hill. Known locally as the Gizibo, (the local pronunciation) a corruption of the word 'Gazebo', it was reportedly erected to give relief work at the time of the famine in 1846-47 However, a local historian tells me it was recorded as being built in 1836 by Colonel Knox who lived at that time in Castlelacken. The ruins of this building lie behind the tall wall passed on the right. Another magnificent view of Lacken Strand unfolds as you top the hill. This is a sand flat of 600 acres (240 Hectares), at low tide and the venue, twice a year, for the Lacken Races where some fine horse racing meetings take place. If you kept to the Wild Atlantic Way however you can see this fine area. Take note that this road

is not really suitable at present for coaches. Six hours later the same strand will be covered by the springing tides powering through the narrow gap known as 'Pullaun na Gur'. Not a safe spot to swim, although the beach at the sea proper is excellent.

The sands can be soft just where the river exits, so this is a spot at low tide near the estuary for cars to keep away from. The strand entry is also a place where on occasion Foróige have held Youth rallies with a gathering upwards of two thousand young people from all over the country.

↖ Lacken strand

Many young aspiring drivers have taken their first drive here, while it is a favourite launching spot for model aircraft. Sand yachting can also be an occupation for young people, and when the tide floods the area it is a great spot for novice windsurfers. Nearby in the local Church there is a lovely stained glass window depicting St Patrick hearing his call to Foghill and his subsequent preaching in the area.

The Castlelacken Piper

Notice that built into the shelter of the hills are the remains of the Castlelacken Demesne. A delightful story is told of a happening there on a summers evening two or three hundred years ago. As the sun disappeared into the west if one had chanced to walk down the road, one might have suddenly heard, caught in the evening breeze, the haunting melodies of a master piper playing his uileann pipes repertoire.

↖ Castlelacken ruins

It would be so, because in the castle the Lord had in his retinue an old, blind piper who for sixty years or more, gathered in his memory a huge collection of tunes. His employer thought so much of his skill that one night when sharing a meal with a friend who also had a piper in his employ, during their recourse, over some drinks he foolishly boasted that nobody could match his piper's skill.

Words led to words and eventually, to settle their argument over who of the two pipers had the most tunes in their repertoire, a large wager was decided upon. In fact to lose was to not only to acknowledge defeat, but also forfeit his estate to the other. A date was set and as the wager became known, a crowd gathered to hear the contest.

You can imagine the scene! The old piper starting off with a probable favourite, a lively tune, 'Miss McLeod's reel', the other piper repeating it faithfully.

The night went on and it became noticeable that there were longer pauses between each tune. As the tension climaxed and the thought of what was at stake hit the owners, the pipers quenched their thirst and sought inspiration from any and every source. The audience would be shouting out encouragement and names of long forgotten tunes only to be told, "yes we played that one."

Eventually as dawn broke the old blind man asked his 'boy', his guide, to lead him out for a breath of air. Outside he confided "that he was beaten" as he had no more tunes. "You must have sir" the young man said. "I have nothing left" was the piper's reply as his head slumped down in defeat. Suddenly he cocked his ear as a skylark rose from the ground in the morning dawn and broke into that glorious series of notes and trills that only a skylark can. Trembling, he carefully lifted his set of pipes and filled the bag with air, set his fingers on the chanter and playing, mimicked the skylark. "Bring me in" he ordered. Sitting down he taunted his opponent. "I bet you can't you play this one" he challenged and broke into the wonderful haunting tune we know of as 'The Lark in the Clear Air', the music soaring and twirling in a faithful replica of the skylark's glorious morning anthem.

His opposite number lined up his instrument and tried in vain. He failed to capture the rhythm and timing of the notes and had to admit he was beaten. Thus was the castle saved and a new tune born. Now if you wish to hear a skylark singing, remember to listen for them at Downpatrick. You may be blessed.

The View Far Away

We shall move on as the view magnificently shows up across the bay, the seaside towns of Enniscrone and Easkey and at least three wind farms helping to lower our CO_2 emissions.

Further to the left, in the distance, in a gap after the range of mountain which has stretched for a long section of the horizon, is Knocknarea, a long and flat mountain which catches the eye.

With good eyesight on a clear day one can pick out the cairn of stones on the top, 35 feet high, marking the burial site of Queen Maeve, the legendary Monarch of Connacht around the time of Fionn MacComhaill.

↖ Ross beach with Benbulbin and Knocknarea mountains, County Sligo, in the far distance

Her faithful soldier Ferdia is recorded in a fight to the death over the brown bull of Cooley. As an aside that long range of mountains is called the 'Ox'. This was a mistake by the map maker as he wrongly interpreted the name Slíabh Gauve. This meant, and should be called the windy mountains. Even further around, the hills of Donegal can be seen. Slíabh League is their highest, and has a nearly sheer cliff at the one man pass. With good visibility it has been said that Errigal can be picked out in the far distance. Speaking of hills of stone, you may have noticed the beautiful stone walls facing the houses in this area.

Most of these stones are quarried in the extensive working of three or more established local businesses. Lacken Stone, which is used extensively all over Ireland comes from here. This local entrepreneurial industry provides employment not only in the quarries but also in the area of traditional stonemasonry. Those of the craft travel quite a distance to produce beautiful examples of this brown and grey stone.

The Fishing Disaster

A short diversion to Lacken pier, which is signposted, would bring you to a spot lovely for swimming when the tide is in. It is also in use by local fishermen. Before salmon fishing was banned when stocks declined, several families made a good living from catching and shipping them off.

Now using lobster and crab pots and then storing their catches in submerged stores for export to the French market are the main occupation for the boats. Lacken was one of the places that tragically suffered in the west coast drowning disasters of 1927. On the 28th October several boats with crews of eight men and operated by oars were out fishing for herring. Suddenly, without warning, hurricane force winds hit. Most of the boats were driven ashore on the back-strand, on the right of the bay and the crews were saved. One was driven on to the rocks and smashed up and one of that crew lost his life. The boat which was the farthest out never made it to land and the crew of eight were lost and bodies never recovered.

A total of 54 fishermen were drowned that terrible night along the west coast from Cleggan in Galway, Inniskea off the Mullet and here. A beautiful local stone memorial at the pier names the men who lost their lives at this location.

Memorial bui
by a nephe
of one of th
casualties. H
carved it fro
Lacken ston

In Loving Memory of
THOSE WHO LOST THEIR LIVES IN
DROWNING DISASTER 28. OCT. 1927.
ANTHONY COOLICAN 23 YEARS
ANTHONY GOLDRICK 19 YEARS
MICHAEL GOLDRICK 31 YEARS
PAT GOLDRICK 40 YEARS
TOM GOLDRICK 40 YEARS
ANTHONY KEARNEY 32 YEARS
MARTIN KEARNEY 33 YEARS
PAT KEARNEY 43 YEARS
TOM LYNOTT 50 YEARS
R. I. P.
The Rose of Lacken

The North Coast & Down

Leaving the Parish of Lacken behind, as we crest the hill locally named the 'Tower', the magnificent vista of the North Mayo coastline opens up.

In the foreground, our target of Downpatrick Head juts out to the sea, rising from the land near sea level, at its base to its extremity where its cliffs tower over an ever-changing sea. Looking on, we see Bunatrahir bay away to the left which is dominated by the refurbished, old, coast guard station now the Stella Maris hotel. Following these is the sweep of cliff and mountain, culminating in the far distance in Benwee Head with its summit point, one thousand and two feet over the sea, over three hundred and fifty feet higher than those at the cliffs of Moher in Co. Clare. The pyramid shaped interpretive centre of the Céide fields is visible in the sunshine and surely catches the eye. Its development and exploration is a credit to Dr. Seamas Caulfield and his team, but that is another interesting story. Do not miss it. Built just at the awesome cliffs of Céide, (pronounced 'Kay'ja') it is a must to explore. Out to sea the pyramid shapes of the Stags (stacks) of Broadhaven point their conical shapes skyward, an unmistakeable mark to seafarers.

éide cliffs with the nterpretive centre in he left foreground. tags of Broadhaven re just visible on the orizon in both views.

Just keep following the Wild Atlantic Way sign until we come to the sign for the 'Down', as Downpatrick is known locally, when once more the Wild-Atlantic-Way sign post appears. Off we go then following them, twisting and turning until we come to gates marking private property. Just before that, note the two dark cave mouths at the inner end of the head. If you line up the right hand one (the landward side), with the dark green spot half way up the headland, a dull reflection of light becomes apparent.

On your return journey you will know the reason why; for this is the landward end of the sea level tunnel which runs right through the headland. What you are seeing is the reflection of light passing through. So we proceed along the roadway, without disturbing either cattle or sheep. We are on private farming property by courtesy of the owners, but following also a path trodden by pilgrims for over sixteen hundred years.

The white spot in th
black rock is actuall
daylight showin
through the caver
Note that it lines u
with the berm show
on top and the whit
spot is sea on botton
and sky on to

The Head and Pul na Sean Tinne

As you turn onto the headland something to catch your eye is one of the many 'Sculpture Trail' inspirations, which we have previously met, on a sculpture route all along North Mayo's north coast.

Officially it represents 'Battling forces' where land and sea struggle for dominance. Practically, we see it as the bow of a boat cresting into a bursting wave and surviving. I suppose this is nearly the same thing. Down on the rocky shore there is treasure indeed for young explorers in the numerous rock pools. Sea anemones abound in vivid colours with little fishes and shrimps darting from one hiding place to another. There is maybe the chance of discovering a lobster hiding in a cleft of the rocks though I have to admit I never found one. Leaving your transport now and moving on, past the car park and on your left are two clefts in the rock. This was dangerous but the work done by the improvements is so noticeable, for the fence is gone and clefts visibly sealed so you can see and hear the breaking seas at the bottom, as you stand over them. This is where the water surges through a rock fault cavern all the way from the outer cliff part of the head.

You will see this much more clearly at the bigger and previously mentioned 'Pul na Sean Tinne' where the roof has collapsed over the cave and the fencing around it hindered viewing access. This has all been magnificently changed by the Wild Atlantic Way work.

Pul na Sean Tinne

Planned by Travis Price a famed American archaeological architect, Dr Seamas Caulfield backed by the National Geographic Society and students from the American Catholic University, a berm of soil was built around it, thus hiding the fencing on the approach and preserving a natural look. A shelter was built and in it are details of the story of the place with a viewing platform on top.

As you look closely at the cavern wall you may see where the rock fault slippage has occurred. If you line up the rock strata, a difference of some eight feet would seem to be what has happened between the left side and the arch. There, in stormy weather and from a distance, the vapour and spray which is sucked up by the wind, as in a natural drawing chimney, is visible. Some refer to it as a blow-hole, but strictly speaking it is not, as water is not restricted and extruded under pressure. It looks like a smoking fire, hence, the translation of 'Pul na Sean Tinne', meaning 'the hole of the old fire'. Sometimes in stormy weather the spume drawn up from this dark, forbidding cavern covers quite a large area in a coating of foam.

You can see the light reflected from the outer side. Kayakers have come right through but reported strong currents, while I know of wetsuit-clad, strong swimmers reaching the hole from the landward end. This was done at slack tide time and is not to be done without notification.

The Tragic Loss of Life

This then is the site of the tragedy recorded for you on the rock memorial of local stone. The history (of it) is that after the 1798 rebellion, which was triggered by the landing of one thousand-one hundred French troops at Kilcummin, supported by many local pikemen, the gallant but forlorn effort was finally put down and as with all conquering armies at that time, the defeated were chased, harried and put to the sword, shot or hanged.

So it was that a little group of local pikemen fleeing from the vengeance of the marauding troops elected to get the help of an old woman to let them down into this fearsome hole. Creeping along the ledges till out of sight of searching eyes they clung to the steep sides of the cave, watching fearfully as the incoming tide encroached upon them. They were hoping in vain that the infantry seeking their lives would go away. It was however, that the woman who had let them down was terrorized and could not get back to drop a rope down in time to allow them escape the unyielding tide. They were swept to their deaths.

The story is told of one of the pursuing soldiers shooting, with his musket, a dog that was present around the area. When asked why he did this, he replied that "the hound would have wanted to be with his master" and so would have given away the hiding place. He probably risked his life by his kind action. This then was but one of the tragic cruelties that took place over two hundred years ago.

↖ This is the seaward end of the cavern through the head.

The Old Christian Church and Folklore

On a more cheerful note, one could move on to the piece of history of Christianity and Saint Patrick. Especially here in Downpatrick, the presence of our Patron Saint is recorded and the outline of what must have been a place of worship or oratory remains.

It stands as a testimony to a very early Christian building and is the site of the annual pilgrimage occurring on the last Sunday of July. Many come to worship our God and Creator as Mass is celebrated. In the beauty and serenity of such a setting it is easy to worship, in awe at the power of His creation. The atmosphere and peacefulness of the spot can draw you very close to the Great Creator. As the hymn writer so aptly puts it "Drop thy still dews of quietness till all our strivings cease. Breathe through the earthquake, wind and fire. O still small voice of peace". An interesting architectural feature of this building, which the experts tell us date to Saint Patrick's era, is the cornerstone arrangement. Normally one would expect to see one square corner stone on top of another thus tying the corner together. Here however, the stones are set at a forty five degree angle to each other, thus completing the square. This is most noticeable at the northern corner. The placing of the stones can be ignored however, as in an effort to tidy and dignify the sides, a group of workers detailed to clean up the site, gathered the loose stones and placed them back as they saw fit. Unfortunately, no historical or archaeological opinion was sought and so their placing remains ironically, out of place.

1968

Dun Briste's Arrival

This then is the site on which is based the lovely old legend of Saint Patrick and the druid Crom Dubh. I have heard many different versions from many different sources, but I shall tell the story as I heard it, as a small boy listening to tales from the Gardener family who reside close to the 'Down'. John Andy has long since passed on to his reward and his family have lived for generations in close proximity. He was a mine of history and information and he told this particular story with great relish.

← The photo to the left was taken in 1968.

The photo to the right was taken in 2015. It shows little erosion since 1968 →

It went as such: Apparently the saint spent some time preaching, by explaining the 'Trinity' with the Shamrock and teaching the local people about Christianity in the area. Being the first time that they would have heard of God's love for humanity, and of the sacrifice of His Son on Calvary that our human sin could be forgiven, there were many who resisted, clinging instead to the pagan teachings of old. Such a fellow was Crom Dubh, a pagan druid who lived on the extremity of the headland, over a rock bridge to where he lived. This druid did everything in his power to harass the preaching of the saint. We can only imagine the frustration and trial that this was to Saint Patrick.

One night he took up his troubles to the Lord in prayer, asking that some sort of division or 'mearing' (an Irish word meaning division) would be put between Crom Dubh and himself. A storm then arose that night and resulted in the collapse of the rock bridge linking the mainland to the druid's dwelling. The subsequent rescue by the saint, of the persecutor from his isolation, resulted in his conversion to Christianity.

Then, having seen the power of the Saints prayer and the kindness in saving him from certain death, he realised that love, not hate, of fellow man was in the core of the Christian faith. The annals of the 'The Four Masters', a history written in the fourteenth and fifteenth centuries, record the collapse in 1393 of a cliff bridge although it is not clear from the text as to the location of such a happening. So you can decide which one was the answer to the Saint's prayer. Maybe there were two rock bridges.

Dún Briste as it is Now

Now just a short distance from the remains of the old building can be seen the breath taking sea stack called Dún Briste (pronounced brish'tya). Words cannot convey the majesty of this mighty rock formation with its layers of stone deposited aeons ago, standing nearly one hundred feet above the waves.

(One semi-official record gives its height at 45 metres and 63 by 23 metres in area and this would put it at nearly 150 feet high). How it withstands the onslaught of storm force winds and the surging waves in the wild, winter weather of the Atlantic is hard to believe. Witness the wave on the front of the book hitting it. On occasion one can find sizeable stones lifted from the sea and deposited on land and yet the local sub aqua divers of this modern age tell us there is as much of the rock stack below sea level as above. In dead calm weather the writer has seen down through the clear water, its rocky formation at least twenty to thirty feet below sea level. As a matter of interest the ordinance survey map shows an area of one rood and thirty nine perches or about one tenth of a hectare.

At the top of the stack, for years, it had been argued that what looked like a human building on the left hand side of the arch was merely a rocky outcrop where the greater black backed gulls perched and dominated the bird life.

In 1986 a televised program of a visit and an investigation by Dr Seamus Caulfield and Dr Martin Downes of the area on top was made. RTE filmed a helicopter landing and leaving tents and victuals for the pair who slept there with others. The helicopter returned twenty four hours later and brought the owners of the rock out to stand on their property. At that stage their inspection proved that there was a building on it, and that it was indeed of human construction. This was shown on television. A broken quern stone leaning against a wall was possibly used as an anchor for a rope tying down the roof in stormy conditions. Tradition has it that a Spanish sea captain flew a kite and got a line over it allowing a sailor to scale and explore the stack. Dún Briste (the broken fort) as it is known, must be one of the most photographed rocks in Ireland. Surprisingly, comparisons of old and new photos show little change in terms of deterioration. If you access the website **www.dunbriste.com** there is a drone-produced video which clearly shows two buildings as well as stunning and dramatic views of the whole outer head produced by kind permission of the named maker.

← Dún Briste looks more robust from the sea view.

Under the surface →

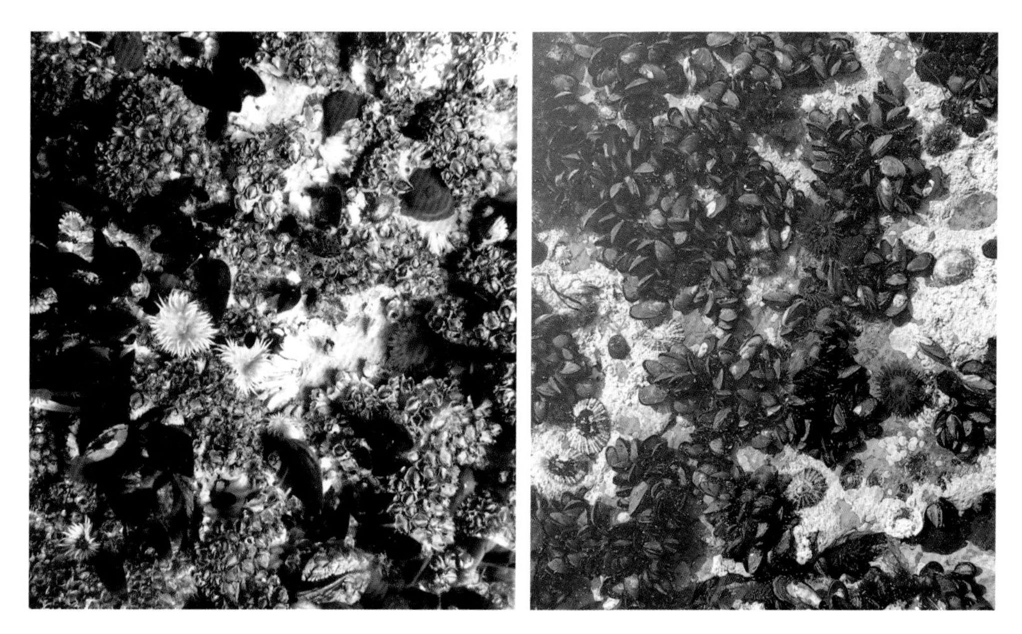

Bird Life and Fauna

There are many varieties of bird life to see like Black Headed and Common Gulls, Gannets, Fulmars, Common and Greater Black Backed Gulls, Kittiwakes and Puffins. Sometimes you may see black foliaged cormorants perched on the rocks holding their wings out to dry after they had been diving for fish.

If you are lucky you may see Choughs, cousins of our jackdaws and crows. Their playful acrobatic flight, with red beaks and black plumage help to identify them.

At nesting time, it is a fascinating sight to see all the different bird species vying for ledge space to lay their eggs. Seabird eggs are very pointed to one end. This helps to stop them rolling off the ledges, as usually there is no nesting material to retain them. They won't roll in a straight direction. It would seem that those clowns of the maritime bird population, the puffins, occupy the lower ledges and then the other species, with a definite demarcation line between each breed, use any of the remaining spaces available. The huge greater black backed gulls lord it over all the others at the top of the stack. The raucous calls, shrieks and general noise are something to experience. It is a fascinating sight to watch the puffins coming in to their nesting places with a beak full of freshly caught sand eels for their chicks and then being harassed and molested by their bigger bullies.

Then when they drop them, the marauder seizing them in mid air, thus thieving from the weaker species. This is a fascinating scene of nature. Lying on the cliff top one can often see the gulls gliding on the up draughts, so close that you can see the feathers control the flight so precisely.

And Flora

Under foot in early summer is a sheet of sea pinks which give such a soft springy surface to walk on. An unusual plant which seems to thrive in the salty conditions of the head is, I am told, the Bucks-horn Plantain.

It is closely related to Ribwort Plantain which produces the seed heads which we called 'soldiers' which in our youth we often played with. Greater plantain, another relative, found on pathways or close mown lawns, has the unique gift of its juice being a quick and certain cure for both bee and wasp stings (acid and alkaline) far superior to the 'dock' leaf that many use. The next time you get a nettle sting you may try it. Another interesting plant noticeable in spring time is Scurvy grass. In spite of its name, it is not a grass and has a noteworthy white flower. Used by sailors as a cure for scurvy, it was valuable before vitamin C present in fruit became a generally known cure.

← The common orchid.

Sea Pinks are also known as thrift →

The Coast Watchers Hut

The derelict hut (once an eyesore in this beautiful spot) dates back to World War II (again it has been refurbished to its original condition by Mayo County Council). At that time all around the coast, a twenty four hour vigil was kept at many points like this by locally enlisted men. They were in communication by telephone with the local Garda station. Interesting, because as a result of war time shortages of copper, the phone line wire connection was simply a single line with earth return, not twin as is normal for phones.

Perhaps this was sufficient to report any unusual sighting but normal conversation or chat would not have been too good. Perhaps Morse code was used. The manning of the post was relieved every eight hours and regardless of rain, storm, darkness or cold, the trail up the head had to be negotiated. At that time Pul na Sean Tinne was not fenced off at all and so the men had a rope strung from pole to pole to guide them on a pitch-black, stormy night. Cold and wet, you can be sure it was great to reach the hut with the turf fire blazing away.

I remember being told of an hourly log being kept, sometimes with little to record. These coast watchers would tell of nights spent in trembling and fear as thundering waves driven by storm force wind would crash against the cliffs throwing spray high in the air over the hut. The solid rock head would shake and vibrate with the furious elements crashing against it and with the knowledge of how the sea had eaten out the underwater passageway, it would be easy for an

imaginative mind to fear the worst. Then there would be long summer days when they would pass time scanning the sea, away to the far horizon for wreckage floating in. Then as happened, a ships lifeboat or a raft or other floating wreckage, the only remaining record of another sinking, would come floating in. Indeed on beaches like Lacken back-strand, timber spars and lumber, barrels of stuff like turpentine and kerosene and even petrol came ashore. They would be claimed by finders keepers, if customs officials didn't get there first. I remember my father being asked to identify a barrel of some unknown liquid, unsuccessfully to the finders disappointment. In hindsight, I believe it was hydraulic fluid with its distinctive smell. Sometimes survivors of the cruel sea would be so glad to be helped to land by local boats. Indeed on occasion, the local cemetery would add another unknown sailor to a quiet corner. The writer remembers seeing a lifeboat of the SS Canton coming ashore and being brought to Kilcummin pier, their crew of 10 or 11 Lascars, as they were described, were suffering from exposure and were hospitalised.

If you are fortunate you may see Basking Sharks, those gentle giants, cruising, even between the stack and head or more likely out to sea. Whale watching has become popular and this is a great place in season for that. Exploring past the hut further to the west side of the head, avoid where the underground tunnel emerges which is especially subject to dangerous collapse. It has a warning rail.

A basking shark. They strain plankton through their wide mouths and are harmless to swimmers ↗

64
EIRE

EIRE 64

Another duty which the coast watchers were detailed to do in the later years of their existence was to monitor the passage of aircraft. Ireland despite having a strictly neutral policy to the belligerents was very complacent towards those using their airspace early in the emergency (this was the Irish name for the Second World War) and they probably saw on occasion, long distance Focke-Wulf Condors or Sunderland aircraft on patrol.

Then there came a time when Flying Fortress bombers were being ferried across the Atlantic, sometimes three or four in a day. They routinely seemed to make landfall near Belmullet. They then used the North Mayo coastline as a guide inland to the RAF base near Enniskillen which is in a nearly straight line. From the early nineteen forties, letting all overflying aircrews know their position over neutral Ireland was aided by setting out in large letters EIRE and nearby a number (on Downpatrick this was 64). This took place all around the coastline at the sites of the Coastwatcher Corps Huts.

The headland on the left shows the earthen fence line. Also a bit on the right which is not sheltered from wave power. Ten centuries of exposure hasn't damaged all of it.

I remember well as a small boy seeing these planes passing, or hear them, hidden by cloud, go over by day. Some days maybe three or four would be recorded.

The Cliff Fort

Sadly in 1940 the stones to create EIRE 64 were removed from the remains of an old cliff fort a couple of hundred yards from the site. One can imagine the Sergeant in charge of the Army platoon delegated to form the letters crying out. "Get on with it boys, this is an easy one. There are plenty of flags (flat-stones) in that old wall over there".

Telling this story to a visiting official, he was amused and laughingly said to me, "Do you know who that Sergeant was?" He was my uncle. Over the past sixty years or so EIRE had practically disappeared under vegetation but has been uncovered as a historic fact, by the hard work of the Wild Atlantic Way supported by Catholic University students from America. Part of the old stone wall still remains. At many sites around the coast these cliff forts were a refuge from marauding Vikings. Livestock and indeed families were quickly hidden behind the walls and the entrance blocked to keep them safe. Dún Aengus (Dún Aonghasa) on Inishmore, the largest of the Aran Islands off Galway Bay, being the most famous and well preserved of these forts. Here in Downpatrick the remains of earthen fences (these were raised barriers of earth) around the cliff edges are just about visible as ridges while the original wall has nearly gone.

ottom left is a
hoto from 1968
f the earthen
ence lines.

You can see these especially on the right hand cliff side where they are well preserved. It is believed that these were to keep livestock, and indeed children, safe. As a small boy I can remember in the existing stone wall a narrow entrance about 40cm wide, and with a right angled wall outside it, only approachable by one attacker at a time, for defence purposes.

The Green Flash

And so our visit to this magnificent and beautiful part of God's creation is nearly over. One last gift which may be viewed from this fabulous place is a chance to see 'The Green Flash'. A phenomenon, usually only seen in tropical places, happens when the sun, on a cloudless summer's evening apparently descends into the sea. At the precise moment when the last rim of that orb leaves our view a magnificent green turquoise flash, nearly florescent in its strength, can be viewed.

To see it from Downpatrick Head, as my wife and I have seen, is a treat indeed, as it is rarely noted in temperate latitudes. It must be emphasised that there must be absolutely no cloud on the horizon for you to view this 'once seen - never forgotten' treat. So your visit to the 'Down' is nearly over. As you leave this tranquil place on a summers evening, let its soothing balm come with you, back to the hectic coming and going of modern life. Breathe a prayer of thankfulness, in a verse of a poem written by Henry Van Dyke which I treasure and have repeated many times. It seems so fitting for this unique place. It's just another thankful soul expressing in a simple way what we find so hard to do; say thanks for the beauty and serenity of the marvellous creation that our loving God has given to us.

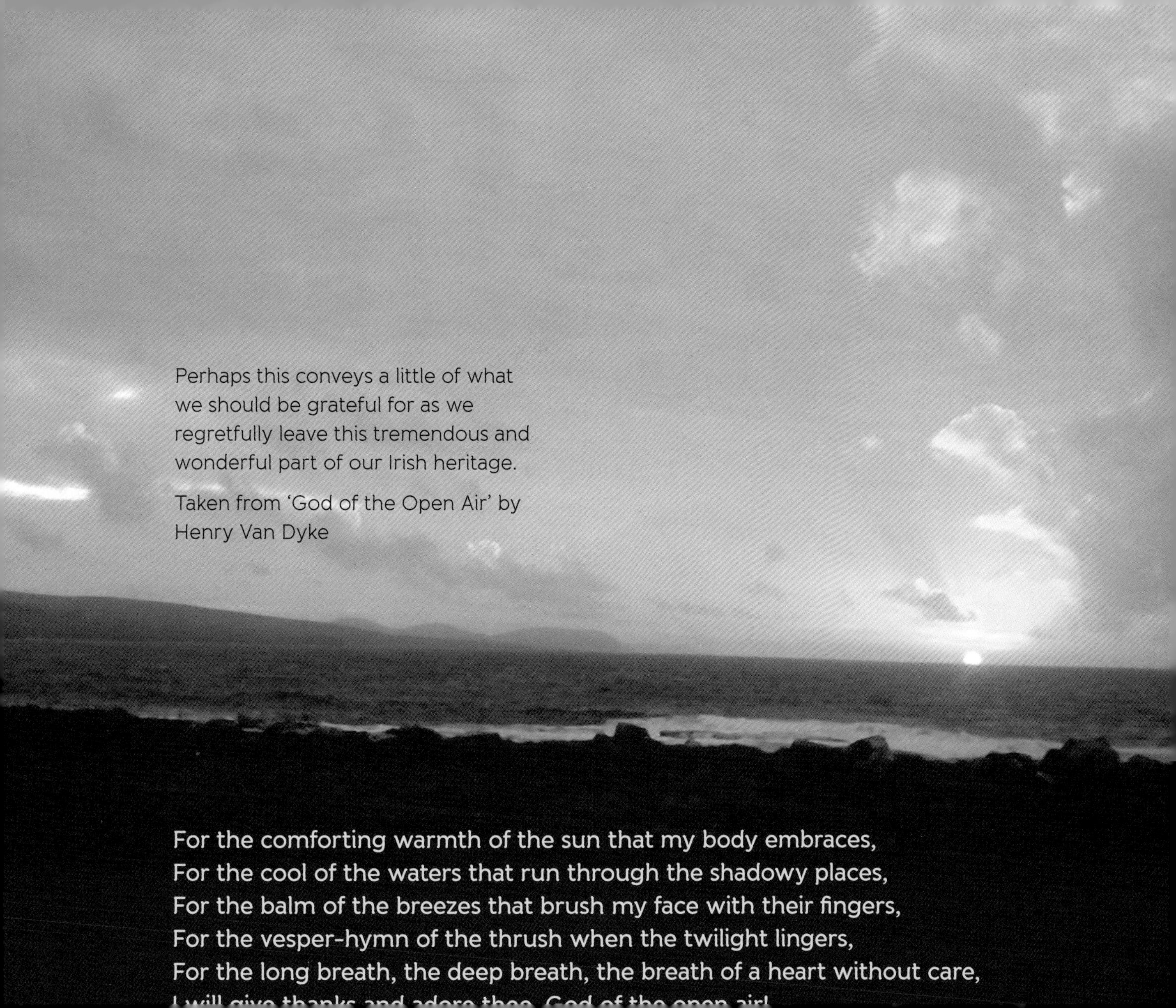

Perhaps this conveys a little of what we should be grateful for as we regretfully leave this tremendous and wonderful part of our Irish heritage.

Taken from ‘God of the Open Air’ by Henry Van Dyke

For the comforting warmth of the sun that my body embraces,
For the cool of the waters that run through the shadowy places,
For the balm of the breezes that brush my face with their fingers,
For the vesper-hymn of the thrush when the twilight lingers,
For the long breath, the deep breath, the breath of a heart without care,
I will give thanks and adore thee, God of the open air!

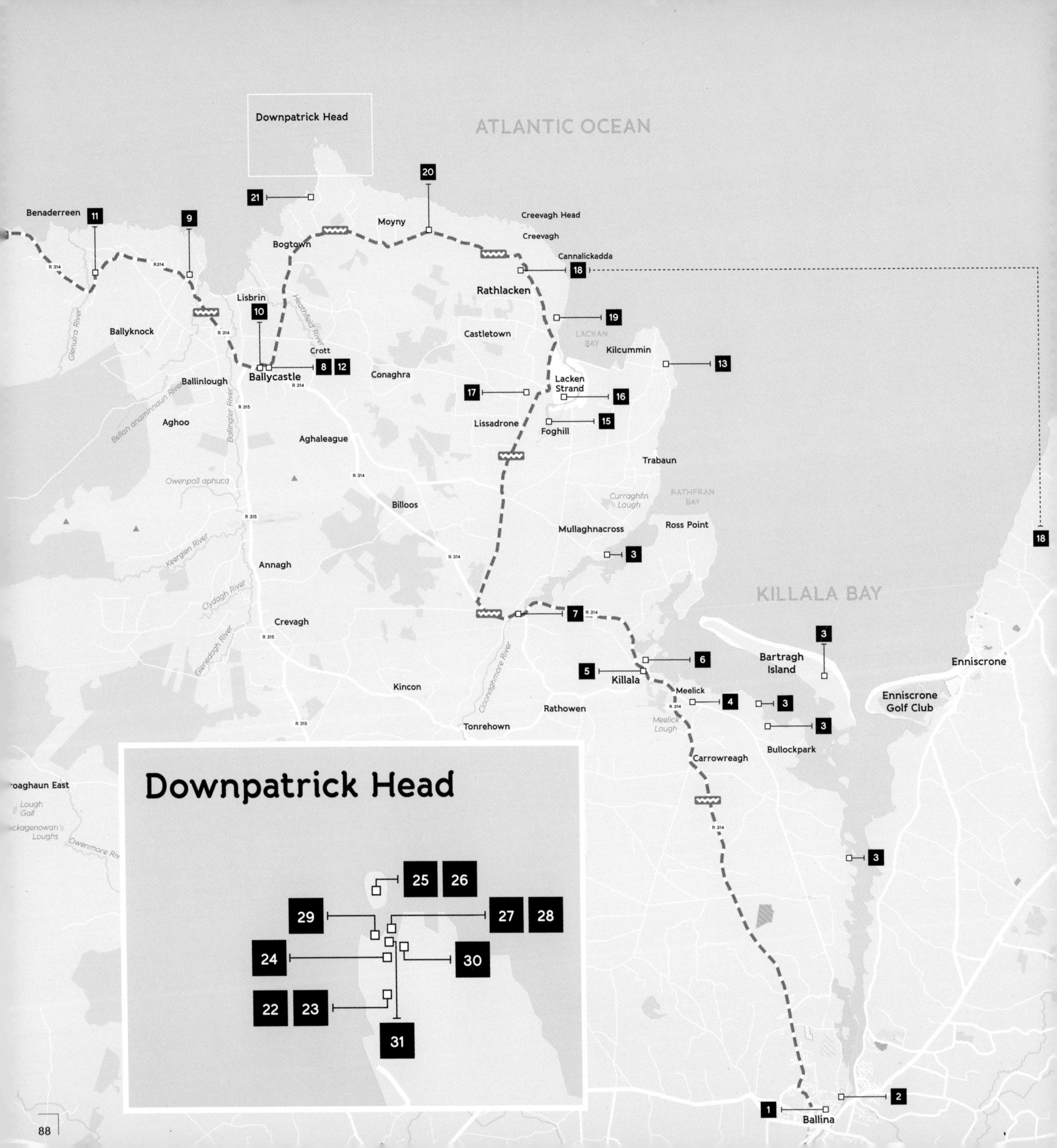
Downpatrick Head
ATLANTIC OCEAN
KILLALA BAY
Benaderreen
Moyny
Creevagh Head
Creevagh
Cannalickadda
Bogtown
Rathlacken
Lisbrin
Ballyknock
Castletown
Kilcummin
Crott
Ballycastle
Conaghra
Ballinlough
Lacken Strand
Aghoo
Lissadrone
Foghill
Aghaleague
Trabaun
Owenpoll aphuca
Billoos
Mullaghnacross
Ross Point
Annagh
Crevagh
Bartragh Island
Enniscrone
Killala
Meelick
Kincon
Rathowen
Tonrehown
Enniscrone Golf Club
Carrowreagh
Bullockpark
Ballina
Downpatrick Head